THE SOUTH DOWNS

THE SOUTH DOWNS

TRAVELS THROUGH WHITE CLIFF COUNTRY · MICHAEL GEORGE

FOREWORD BY
DENIS HEALEY

PARKGATE
BOOKS

First published in 1992

This edition published in 1998 by
Parkgate Books Ltd
Kiln House
210 New King's Road
London SW6 4NZ
Great Britain

9 8 7 6 5 4 3 2 1

First published by Pavilion Books in 1992 at £14.99

British Library Cataloguing in Publication Date:
A catalogue record for this book is available from the British Library.

ISBN 1 85585 532 1

Printed and bound in China
by Sun Fung Offset Binding Company Limited.
Produced in association with the Hanway Press, London.

Page 1: Cooden beach
Page 3: Pevensey Bay

All the photographs for this book were taken with Kodachrome 64 film. The author is
deeply grateful to Kodak Limited for its generous support of the project.

The Roman fort of Anderida at Pevensey, built in the third century on a spit of land projecting into a lagoon, and abandoned in 410, fell to the invading Ælle in 491, from which year, according to the *Anglo-Saxon Chronicle*, can be dated his ascendancy as King of the South Saxons (from which the county name of Sussex derives). Overnighting within the ten acres enclosed by the Romans, following his landing near here, William, Duke of Normandy hastily erected one of two portable castles which he had brought with him, before marching on Hastings. In 1940, when the so-called 'Saxon shore' again came under attack by Germanic hordes, the Roman walls once more provided cover for British defenders.

ACKNOWLEDGEMENTS

Gillon Aitken, Aitken & Stone Limited; Brian Allchorn, Allchorn Pleasure Boats; Kitty and Michael Ann, Drusillas Park; Jean and Roger Antrobus; The Association of Photographers: Janet Ibbetson, General Secretary; BAPLA, British Association of Picture Libraries and Agencies: Sal and Brian Shuel; Bexhill Careers Office: Judith Pearson and Marjorie Blatchly; Bexhill Photographic: Sid O'Laughnane; Berwick Parish Church of St Michael and All Angels: The Revd Peter Smith, Rector, and Robert Carpenter, Churchwarden; The Booth Museum of Natural History: Dr Gerald Legg, Keeper of Biology; Brighton Borough Council, Parks and Recreation Department: Mike Griffin, Director, and David Ford, Senior Countryside Ranger; Brighton Borough Council, Tourism and Resort Services Department: William Burnett, MBE, Director, and Jan Cadge, Personal Assistant; Rosemary Bryant; Margaret and John Chapman; Kay Challoner; the Revd Richard Chapstick, Vicar, the Chapel Royal, Brighton; Charleston Farm: The Charleston Trust, Christopher Naylor, Director, Linda Field and Francette Lyons); Charleston Manor: Julia and Peter Kandiah; *Country Life*: Jenny Greene, Editor; *Country Living*: Miranda Innes, Garden Editor, and

Georgina Rhodes, Consultant Art Director; CPRE, Council for the Protection of Rural England (Sussex Area): Dr Peter Brandon, Chairman; Howard Davies; Neil Diment; Ian Dunnett; East Sussex County Council: Joan M Mont, Chairman, and Ann Thomas, assistant; East Sussex County Council Planning Department, Countryside Management Service: Paul Millmore, Countryside Management Officer, Mark Hayward, Brighton-Hove Downland Ranger, Romy Luffman and Norman Brown; East Sussex County Record Office: Judith and Colin Brent; Eastbourne Borough Council, Planning and Technical Services Department: George Williams, Director, David Haizelden, Manager, and Alan Ferguson, Downland Ranger; Eastbourne Tourism & Leisure: Ronald G Cussons, Director of Tourism & Leisure, Mark Smith and Penny Waugh; *L'École de Cuisine Française* – Sabine de Mirbeck: Sabine de Mirbeck-Brassart, Director, and Audrey Horlock, Secretary; FAU, Field Archaeology Unit, Institute of Archaeology: Dr Peter L Drewett, Director, and David R Rudling, Deputy Director; Dr John M Fritz; Firle Place: The Rt Hon the Viscount Gage, Hazel Gage, the Showing Secretary, and Penny and Peter Woolgar; Folkington Place: Hendrick Voorspuy, and

Priscilla Coventry; Friston Place: The Rt Hon Lord Shawcross, GBE, QC, William Shawcross, and Elaine and Michael Franks; Megan and Eric George; Glynde Place: The Rt Hon the Viscount Hampden; Alexander Gray: David Gray, Barry Wright, Jean Anderson, and Joan Lundy; Donald L Hillegas; Penelope Hoare; Dr Malcolm Hooker; John Houghton; Jim Howell, Clerk & Chief Fisheries Officer, Sussex Sea Fisheries District; Impact Photos: Liz Moore, Managing Director, Hilary Genin, Library Manager, and Philippe Achache; the *Independent* Newspaper Publishing PLC: Christopher McKane, Picture Editor, Keith Dobney, Deputy Picture Editor, and Victoria Lukens, Picture Desk; Robert Jacobs and Terry Dalton, Délifrance, Eastbourne; Julian Ford Bird Sanctuary: Sue and Julian Ford; Libby Ketchum, The Conservation Foundation; Kodak Limited, Professional Photography Division: Michael George, Manager, and Paul Gates, Press and Trade Relations; Lewes Citizens Advice Bureau: Dick Myers; Lewes District Council, Leisure Services Department: Terry Powell, Director of Leisure Services, and Mandy Jameson, Marketing and Promotions Officer; John Lister; Bernhard Living; Sebastian Loew; Christopher Lynch; the Revd

Peter Markby, Rector, St John's Church, Southover, Lewes; Councillor Dr Graham Mayhew; Allen Meredith; *Metropolitan Home*: Celia Goodrick-Clarke, Assistant Editor; Dr George Michell; Francine and Ivor Miskin, Kall-Kwik Printing, Eastbourne; The National Gardens Scheme Charitable Trust (East & Mid-Sussex): Yvonne Toynbee, Hon County Organizer; The National Trust for Places of Historic Interest or Natural Beauty, Kent & East Sussex Regional Office: Caroline Mayell, Assistant Land Agent, and Glen Redman, National Trust Warden, Crowlink; Newhaven Port: Captain Alec Flint, Harbour Master; Normec: David Gould, Director, Steve Tyrell, Director, Marshall Grey, and Carol Moon; Offham House: Anne and Sandy Goodman; Olympus Optical Co. (U.K.) Limited: Graeme Chapman, Marketing Director, Ian Dickens, General Manager, Consumer Division, Catherine Fowler and Robin Hinton; Pevensey Castle: English Heritage (Historic Buildings & Monuments Commission); Dorothea and Robert Powter; The Revd Keith Richards, Vicar, the Church of St Margaret, Rottingdean; The Royal Pavilion Art Gallery and Museums, Brighton: Dr Richard Marks, Director, and Ann Kenny, Head of Public Services; The

Royal Photographic Society: Michael Austin, President, Amanda Nevill, Carol Agar and Tony Tracy FRPS; Constance B Sayre; Seven Sisters Country Park: Mike Guy, Monty Larkin and Peter Dodsley; Audrey and Michael Smith; The Society of Authors: Kate Pool, Assistant General Secretary (Contracts); Society of Sussex Downsmen: Fergus Huddleston, General Secretary, Brian Sims, Hon Membership Secretary, Derek Langston-Jones, District Officer, and Michael Isitt, District Officer; Michele Spencer; Spiral Staircase Systems, Glynde: Colin Sullivan, Tyl Kennedy and Angie Van Tilborg; Abner Stein. The Sussex Archaeological Society: Andrew Pepper, Chief Executive, and Janet France, Membership Secretary; Jane Thorp, Manager, W H Smith & Son Limited, Bexhill-on-Sea; Dr Erica Towner, Lecturer in Biological Science, Centre for Continuing Education, University of Sussex; Kevin Traverse-Healy, Managing Director, Charles Barker Traverse-Healy, Public Relations; Joan Vann; Maureen Venton; Charles Wardle, MP; Peter Weston; Janet Williams; the Revd Canon and Mrs Horace James Woodward; Ilsa Yardley; YHA Adventure Shops PLC, Brighton: Angela Curtis.

CONTENTS

Lᴵᴷᴱ ᴹᴬɴʏ ᴀ Northerner working in London, I tended to go south to the sun and sea when I could get away. I settled at Alfriston towards the end of my stint as Chancellor of the Exchequer, partly because I found the Cuckmere valley so attractive; its hills are tawny rather than green, reminding me of my beloved Yorkshire Dales. So for more than ten years I have lived at the heart of the white cliff country which Michael George has recorded so well in this book.

The downland of East Sussex is unique in Britain. Air and sky are its essence. Its cloudscape is as beautiful as its landscape. Rudyard Kipling captured the loveliness of 'our blunt, bow-headed, whale-back downs' in four lines.

> Bare sloped, where chasing shadows skim,
>   And through the gaps revealed
> Belt upon belt, the wooded, dim
>   Blue goodness of the Weald.

It is a land of harmonious contrasts, with a special appeal to every type of visitor. Brighton has been England's first and most fashionable seaside resort since Prinny built the Royal Pavilion. It has changed little since Horace Smith described it in those days:

> The Cit foregoes his box and Turnham Green,
>   To pick up health and shells with Amphitrite;
> Pleasure's frail daughters trip along the Steyne,
>   Led by the dame the Greeks call Aphrodite.
> Loose trousers snatch the wreath from pantaloons:
>   Nankeen were worn the sultry weather in;
> But now (so with the Prince's Light Dragoons)
>   White jean have triumphed o'er their Indian brethren.

I suppose the only difference today is that pantaloons and Indian wear are back again, the jeans are blue, and Pleasure has some frail sons as well as daughters in the Lanes.

Before the first world war the Downs attracted the perhaps over-hearty virility of Kipling and Belloc. In the interwar period it appealed to the ambiguous sensitivity of the Bloomsbury set, who left Charleston farmhouse and Monks House at Rodmell as permanent memorials – not to speak of the frescoes at Berwick Church.

East Sussex has survived many invaders – Roman, Saxon, Dane, French and German. Not all the invaders have been hostile; Debussy wrote *La Mer* at the Grand Hotel in Eastbourne. The invaders nowadays are from all over the world and of all ages – Eastbourne attracts the old, and Brighton the young; whole families, from toddlers to grandparents, pass over the cliff walks between Seaford and Beachy Head.

The core of East Sussex is the top of the Downs which are vibrant with beauty and with mystery at all seasons and all times of day. I know a spot on the path above the Long Man of Wilmington from which you can see a great 180° arc of sea, stretching from Hastings to Selsey Bill.

Before the second world war, ribbon development spoiled much of the coast from Newhaven to Brighton. Since the war, cattle and cereals have too often replaced the traditional sheep whose grey curves fit perfectly in the landscape. And the yellow curse of rape-fields sometimes blights the 'blue goodness of the Weald'.

But the essence of the Downs remains. Not just the sky and the sea and vast expanses of high country which has not changed in two thousand years, but also the chalkland flowers, the waterbirds and skylarks, and the flintstone walls of cottage, church and barn. All these are lovingly immortalised by Michael George's camera. We must make sure that they remain the same for future generations to enjoy.

Denis Healey

Three of George III's children came on holiday to 'East-bourne', thus helping to make it a fashionable watering place. However, the future character of the resort, nestled beneath the Downs, was largely determined by the lord of the manor, William Cavendish, later seventh Duke of Devonshire, who began to develop it in stately fashion in 1851. During the Second World War Eastbourne was chosen by the enemy as a target for constant bombardment, the heaviest sustained by any town in the south-east. Between the summer of 1940 and the spring of 1944 there were 98 raids, over 1,000 civilian casualities (174 fatal), and enormous damage was done to property.

THROUGHOUT HISTORY, CLOSE proximity to the Continent combined with its long coastline to make White Cliff Country exceptionally vulnerable to attack: in succession, Celts, Romans, Saxons and Normans have swept past the great bulwark of chalk to leave their mark on the rolling hills behind.

Within a few short years of the withdrawal, in 410, of the Roman legions from the shore that they had strongly defended against the Saxons, the *litus Saxonicum,* the Celtic inhabitants of Britain found themselves powerless to resist the advance of land-grabbing Germanic hordes, who had no hesitation in regarding the people they ruthlessly displaced as foreigners or *wealas* (Welsh). So relentless were the Saxons in carving kingdoms for themselves, and so pervasive was the influence of their English tongue, that east of a line from the Yorkshire wolds to Southampton there is precious little evidence of British survival, even in the names of the rivers.

In 485, a fierce but indecisive engagement in the long struggle for supremacy took place, according to the *Anglo-Saxon Chronicle,* at Mercredes burn (from Welsh *môr* meaning 'sea' and *rhyd* meaning 'ford', hence, in all probability, Seaford). Some six years later, at Andredes ceaster (the Roman fort of Anderida, now Pevensey), the invaders 'slew all that dwelt therein, nor was there one Briton left'.

In this kingdom of the South Saxons (Sussex) thus established by Ælle, the leader of the whole English movement against the Britons of the South, a sea of Saxon place names washed out all trace of the British except, ironically, the word 'Downs', from Celtic *dún,* meaning either a 'hill' or a 'fort' (at times, of course, it was necessarily both). Only the hatching of a Celtic field system on the side of one of these hills or the whorl of a hill fort built on its summit provide eloquent testimony to their formerly British character.

As one whose ancestors were branded foreigners (Welsh), and hemmed in by intruding barbarians in the upland of West Britain, I have felt an affinity for the East Sussex hills, or 'mountains', as they were romantically described by the English naturalist Gilbert White. So that, even after living for several years amidst the alien peaks and canyons of Manhattan I experience a sense of homecoming in Downland.

In a curious reversal of a trend forced on the Celts over a thousand years ago, my parents migrated from Wales to the Saxon shore shortly after it had been, once again, the frontline under German attack. By what species of atavistic impulse were we drawn to

Bishopstone in 1945, so close to the scene, in 485, of one of the great turning points in our collective history?

Without a feeling of connectedness to the past, it is virtually impossible to appreciate any landscape, especially that of the East Sussex hills, where so much of England's early history was enacted. Here, after all, the fate of the nation was decided, on 14 October 1066, when, following their unopposed landing at Pevensey, William, Duke of Normandy and his army of iron-fisted, greedy adventurers completed one of the quickest conquests ever recorded.

But perhaps the most influential of all immigrants were among the first to arrive on the East Sussex shore: the Neolithic herdsmen with their grazing stock and cereal crops who, beginning about five thousand years ago, cleared the primeval forest and created a pattern of husbandry that was to define both the contours and the fortunes of the chalk hills on which they settled.

This elevated hinterland of well-rounded chalk, a roughly triangular area bounded by Brighton in the west, Eastbourne in the east and Lewes at the apex, coincides with the extent of the South Downs as they were famously perceived, in about 1800, by the Revd Arthur Young, the influential writer on agriculture, who was amazed to discover no fewer than 200,000 ewes browsing 'a very short, sweet and aromatic herbage, peculiar to these hills'.

Like so many of the classic features of the English landscape, the sheep-cropped, species-rich, springy turf which gave the region its celebrated profile, 'so noble and so bare', only existed as a result of the intervention of man.

In this century the Sussex hill farmer has largely abandoned the immemorial usage of the chalk upland for grazing sheep in favour of the intensive cultivation of cereal and fodder crops. As a consequence, the Downs have changed more in the last forty years than they did in the preceding thousand, with one of the most ecologically distinctive habitats on earth now reduced to an estimated five per cent of its original reach.

However, at its core, the East Sussex hills retain the ancient powers of magic and of mystery which have been a consolation and an inspiration to countless generations of people, among them such artists as Rudyard Kipling and Virginia Woolf.

While she discounted the possibility of a beneficent Nature and, at times, despaired of

Piers are a peculiarly English kind of folly. They were built solely for pleasure, and their principal attraction, the sensation of walking on the deck of a ship, could be had without any of the normally attendant expense and inconvenience.

The 1,000-foot pier at Eastbourne, opened in 1872, was designed by Eugenius Birch, doyen of Victorian Britain's pier constructors, to enhance the town's two-and-a-half mile seafront.

Curiously, it was built on the site of a Roman villa, one of only five known to have existed in the county.

'the smug suburbanity of Sussex', Woolf, like Kipling before her, found her adopted hills to be a real balm in periods of anguish. In a letter dated 2 November 1938 to Vanessa Bell, her sister and near neighbour in the country, she wrote: 'Yes, I think landscape a great support. Who prop in these dull days my mind? Well the downs and the River Ouse . . . in spite of the man who shot himself and the sheep I found on its back'.

To Kipling the special genius of the place must have been revealed in 1882, on the occasion of his first visit to 'North End House', the summer home in Rottingdean of his 'beloved aunt' Georgiana ('Georgie') and 'Uncle Ned' (the great pre-Raphaelite painter Sir Edward Burne-Jones). In *Something of Myself* he later recalled that 'the Downs poured almost direct into the village street and lay out eastward unbroken to Russia Hill above Newhaven'.

Just as Kipling was obliged by charabancs bearing celebrity-seekers from Brighton to flee, after only five years' residence, from his own home at 'The Elms' in Rottingdean, so that wild and lovely stretch of coastal Downland which he so admired has been forced to give way to a hopelessly ugly agglomeration of mean, squat bungalows.

From the security of their perch on a groyne near the pier these birds survey the waterfront at Eastbourne.

When he first settled in East Sussex, in 1897, Kipling had, as T. S. Eliot put it, 'both the humility to subdue himself to his surroundings, and the freshness of vision of a stranger'. On Gilbert White the power of suggestion exerted by 'that chain of majestic mountains' never failed, despite an acquaintance of 'upwards of thirty years', to deliver 'new beauties' each time he traversed it.

Few of us, perhaps, are fortunate enough to really see a place – as if for the first time – in such a way that its essential quality, communicating itself clearly to us, becomes an inseparable part of our being.

When out walking on the Downs, I never cease to marvel, whatever the season, at the infinite variation of light modelling White's 'gentle swellings and smooth fungus-like protuberances'. Whereas others may seek present aesthetic pleasure in the contemplation of purely plastic form, my own appreciation of the hill country, so heavily imprinted by man, is shadowed by a melancholy sense, particularly at twilight, of the transience of all things human.

Michael George
East Sussex 1991

As the boarded-up windows
reveal, the old Albion Hotel
on Eastbourne's seafront has
fallen on hard times and faces an
uncertain future.

The Queen's Hotel, opposite the pier in Eastbourne, is one of several stellar hostelries on Marine Parade which can accommodate visitors to the resort with commanding views of the sea.

This gathering on the esplanade at Eastbourne might serve to reinforce the impression of the town as a rather dowdy 'Empress of Watering Places'. However, the number of low-cost housing developments which now cling to the dowager's skirts has led to an increase in the number of young families in the town. The retired population has fallen from two-and-a-half times the national average to one-and-a-half.

At the Battle of Beachy Head, on 30 June 1690, the combined English and Dutch fleets of fifty-six sail, under the command of the Earl of Torrington, engaged the French fleet of eighty-two, under the Comte de Tourville.

Although the superior French force prevailed at sea, the expected Jacobite rising on land did not materialize.

Had Louis XIV succeeded in his attempt to counter the Glorious Revolution of 1688 by restoring the Catholic James II, Britain would have been placed under French patronage and under the religious authority of Rome.

The distinctive red-and-white striped lighthouse was built on the shore half a mile west of Beachy Head at its highest point. The bold headland which dominates it presents a conspicuous staging post for numerous land birds on their annual migrations, while the cliffs themselves are the vertiginous habitat of a variety of sea birds.

Beachy Head had long enjoyed an unenviable reputation as a graveyard for mariners before acquiring its first lighthouse, a small wooden structure, in 1828. Both it and the present stone building which replaced it in 1834, were erected on the curious hill, known as Belle Tout, within a prehistoric earthwork – the remains of an embanked settlement of the Bronze Age, from which domestic artefacts have been recovered. Much of the site has since fallen into the sea, while the lighthouse, now incorporated into a private dwelling, was superseded in 1902 by the one built on the shore to the east.

An alternative beginning to the long-distance footpath known as the South Downs Way traces a route over Beachy Head through some of the most wonderful scenery of the south coast. There are breathtaking glimpses of sheer white precipices and occasional peeks at the boldly sited lighthouse on the shore below.

Operated automatically since 1983, the 880,000 candelas light, with its huge revolving lens, casts a beam which can reach up to twenty-five miles away.

A study in white-on-white was made one February morning, when the residue of a severe snow-storm encrusted the chalk cliff top to the west of Beachy Head lighthouse.

24

Since 1861 the family firm of Allchorn has operated their 'B.O.T. Approved Pleasure Boat Service' seven days a week between May and October, 'wind and weather permitting'. Thus, over the years, untold numbers of visitors to Eastbourne have tested for themselves the proposition that 'the true magnificence of Beachy Heady can only be appreciated from the sea'.

A master of the strangely veering winds and currents off Eastbourne's great headland, Bill Wood, skipper of the *William Allchorn*, and commentator Andrew Todd navigate the difficult passage round the white cliffs, to the unfailing delight of all those who venture on the seven-mile, forty-five-minute cruise to Beachy Head.

The Beachy Head Lighthouse is seen in true perspective from the water. Beginning in 1899, foundations 18 feet deep were dug for the 153-foot beacon. Both men and materials had to be lowered in baskets on an aerial ropeway from the cliff top in order to build the tower, in which pre-cut blocks of Cornish granite, each weighing up to five tons, were used. Since 1902, when the light first shone, the Beachy Head Lighthouse has been a vital link in the chain of 85 lighthouses around the coasts of England and Wales, and an indispensable aid to shipping in the English Channel, one of the world's busiest seaways.

The sea has always figured prominently in the fortunes of East Sussex, whose shore is among the longest of any county in England. Over a period of some 30 million years, when warm subtropical water bathed the entire area, a steady build-up on the sea bed of coccoliths (the calcareous parts of minute planktonic algae) hardened to make the broad band of chalk which, subsequently uplifted and then breached by the English Channel, is now exposed by the sea between Brighton and Eastbourne. The tall, white cliffs to the east of Seaford, culminating in the dramatic promontory of Beachy Head, form one of the most magnificent stretches of untouched coastline remaining in Great Britain.

Arable farming on the 488-acre Bullock Down Farm, one of four contiguous farms which, together with Beachy Head, make up the 4,100 acres of Eastbourne Downland that were acquired by Eastbourne Corporation from the Chatsworth Estate, between 1926 and 1931, at a cost of £91,000. Modern farm practices and poor management have combined to work against the public interest as defined by the Corporation in its original undertaking to preserve the Downland. Ploughing has reduced ecologically rich habitats and damaged some archaeological sites, while fencing has restricted access, thus increasing the pressure from the million visitors a year to the headland itself, one of the few surviving areas of original chalk turf.

High on a hill overlooking Bramble Bottom, to the east of New Barn, stands an old shepherd's cottage, the only listed building on Eastbourne Downland.

In about 1800, the Revd. Arthur Young, the influential writer on contemporary agricultural practice, counted 'the amazing number' of 200,000 ewes on the South Downs between Eastbourne and Steyning, which he considered 'one of the most singular circumstances in the husbandry of England'.

By about 1900 this centuries-old form of land management, which had helped create and sustain the chalk grassland that was typical of the region, had begun to yield in favour of cereal and fodder crops. It is estimated that as much as 95 per cent of old chalk grassland in Sussex has now been destroyed.

New Barn, a good example of this characteristic building type, with, in the background, the old shepherd's cottage, an even more endangered species.

The last rays of fitful sunlight accent a field of rape beneath storm clouds gathering over Went Hill. In an ancient dry valley named for Beor, a Saxon sea-rover who is thought to have settled here, Birling Manor Farm houses a sheep centre where, at different times of the year, visitors may see lambing, shearing and milking, and can watch the making of sheep yoghurt and cheese.

The chalk hills of East Sussex are heavily imprinted by early man, but many of the known sites have been lost in recent years owing to modern farming techniques. This ploughed-out Bronze Age round barrow at Cornish Farm on Eastbourne Downland was erected within sight of the embanked settlement of that period which has been discovered near Belle Tout Lighthouse. The dig, directed by Dr Peter Drewett as a training exercise for students at the Institute of Archaeology, revealed, among other things, the remains of a crouched female in her early thirties.

From Lookout Hill, the most recent addition to the National Trust's substantial holdings in the area, one can appreciate the gracious dipping line of the Seven Sisters. (There are, in fact, an unalliterative eight: Went Hill, Baily's Hill, Flat Hill, Flagstaff Point, Brass Point, Rough Brow, Short Brow and Haven Brow.) The first two sisters form part of the Trust's Crowlink property, which stretches from Friston church to the sea. Founded in 1895 'for the preservation of places of historic interest or natural beauty', the National Trust today is Britain's largest landowner after the Crown, and the country's biggest conservation organization. With the support of its two million members, it protects one-third of the coastline – 516 of a targeted 900 miles – and half a million acres of countryside.

Almost completely hidden from view by the fall of the land surrounding it and well screened by trees, Friston Place occupies a fold in the hills that was probably settled by a Saxon named Becca, as its former name, 'Bechington' (from 'Becca's tun'), reveals.

The beautifully moulded Tudoresque brick chimney and the mullioned and transomed windows, seen from the garden, are among the later additions to a house which is medieval at its core. The magnificent Great Hall, built in Henry VIII's reign, is one of the finest in the country. This jewel of a dwelling is the home of the Rt Hon Lord Shawcross GBE, QC, a past president of the Society of Sussex Downsmen, and one of the county's most distinguished citizens.

The magic of the unspoilt stretch of coastline known as the Seven Sisters resides in its loneliness and wild desolation. Here on Flat Hill, with a tempest raging out to sea, the sheep continue to crop the salt-sprayed turf, with only the mournful cries of wheeling seabirds to disturb them. Until well into the nineteenth century, the gaps in the cliffs at Crowlink and Birling provided secluded access to the sea for 'free traders' bringing in, without payment of customs and excise, tea, tobacco and spirits. At 'the centre of Sussex free trade', as Crowlink was known, there were often running battles over the right to bring in 'Genuine Crowlink', the duty-free gin of the day.

The tapering branches of a bare beech tree reach out and touch the chalky surface of this field above Jevington.

The charmingly secluded village of Jevington takes its name from a Saxon leader (*Jeva*), who obtained for his tribe (*ing*) a settlement (*ton*) in this ancient dry valley in the chalk hills. In the eighteenth and nineteenth centuries, the village, long associated with the breeding of horses, was heavily implicated in the prevailing black economy based on smuggling contraband goods from Crowlink and Birling Gap.

A bank of bluebells, one of the enduring symbols of the British spring, greets the visitor to Jevington in April.

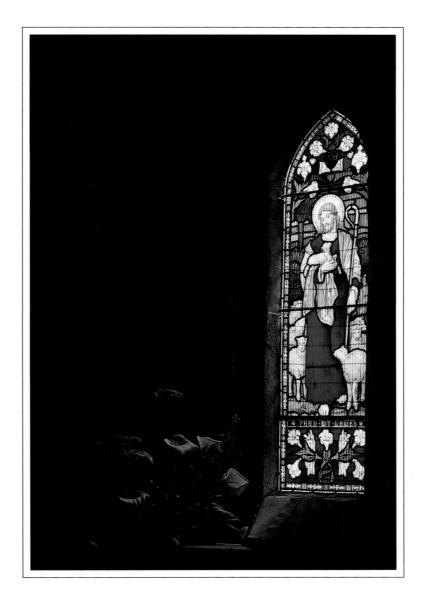

In Jevington parish church Easter lilies form part of the ritual celebration of the life and work of the Good Shepherd. Easily the most remarkable representation of Christ in the church, discovered when the second stage of the belfry was re-floored in 1875, is the Saxon sculpture now set in the north wall of the nave. The sturdy tower, which dates from about 900, may have served the villagers as a defended place of refuge during the period of the Viking raids. Dedicated to St Andrew, patron saint of fishermen, the church was over-restored in the nineteenth century.

If it is true, as Rudyard Kipling noted, that 'no tender-hearted garden crowns' the chalk hills about which he wrote so feelingly, at Folkington Place, above Polegate, the late Mrs Hendrik Voorspuy, with the expert assistance of Miss Priscilla Coventry, came as close as one can get, perhaps, to creating a corner of paradise on the Downs. Working with inherited walls, of brick, some cobble paths, a few Irish yews and a couple of apple trees, they made a garden in which many native wild flowers were given pride of place. The papery-petalled, July-flowering Californian Poppy (*Romneya coulteri*) is a particular favourite of Miss Coventry, who still tends the garden, although now in her eighties.

The common yew (*Taxus baccata*) has great powers of regeneration and has therefore always been a symbol of immortal life. So it is not surprising to learn that, according to local tradition, the body of a Saxon chieftain lies buried under the yew at Wilmington. The immense, twin-stemmed, female tree, estimated to be about 1,400 years old, stands, buttressed and chained, close to the restored fifteenth-century porch of the parish church of St Peter and St Mary. This interesting church once formed part of the adjacent Benedictine priory that was given to Robert of Mortain, legitimate half-brother of the Conqueror, when he took control of the Rape of Pevensey, in which Wilmington is situated, as his Sussex share of the spoils.

While it is not known who cut the figure in the turf, the 240-foot high outline of the Long Man of Wilmington, the most celebrated of the chalk hill figures in England – and the largest representation of a human being in Western Europe – is possibly a Middle Neolithic creation of about 3,200 BC. It has been argued from the 'full-frontal' evidence of the priapic Cerne Abbas Giant in Dorset that, because of Victorian prudery, the Long Man may have 'lost' his male attributes when he was reclaimed for posterity in the late nineteenth century.

The steep north-facing escarpment of the South Downs, here seen in profile from the shoulder of Windover Hill, is one of the most striking topographic features of the region. From the break in the hills at Cuckmere Gap it is possible to get a better idea of their depth from north to south than it is looking up at them from the Weald. Sideways-on, Firle Beacon, at 712 feet above sea level one of the highest points on the ridge, puts one in mind of Kipling's 'blunt, bow-headed, whale-backed Downs'.

From Windover Hill, which at 699 feet above sea level is another of the high points on the northern edge of the Downs, there are breathtaking views of the continuing line of hills and of the Weald laid out below. For much of the South Downs Way, which follows the ridge for about eighty miles to Winchester, the path coincides with a track that was in use, perhaps, two thousand years before the Romans arrived. Windover Hill is one of the most powerful memorials to early man: on its summit are several barrows, or burial mounds, while from the hillside the giant chalk figure of the Long Man of Wilmington 'looks naked towards the shires'.

England's yellow peril, oil-seed rape (*Brassica napus*), consolidates its noisome hold on fields below the northern escarpment of the Downs at Windover Hill. Thanks to price support from the European Commission, this brash contribution to our traditionally well-modulated spring palette is likely to arrest our senses for several seasons to come. In Britain there are now a million acres under rape, roughly 8 per cent of its crop area and 2 per cent of its total farmland.

Between 3,000 and 1,800 BC, semi-nomadic settlers cleared small areas of woodland for grazing and the cultivation of wheat on the chalk just south of Windover Hill.

Not far from the Neolithic long barrow on Fore Down, at Lullington Heath, the Department of the Environment maintains a unit to monitor low-level ozone, the major hazard caused mainly by the reaction of car exhaust fumes to bright sunlight.

In recent years the level of summer air pollution registered has been unacceptably high, as plumes of ozone-rich air have been blown across the country south of London.

In Alfriston, a publicity-seeking swan attempts to divert attention from the centuries old scene described by this meander in the Cuckmere to the south of the parish church and Old Clergy House.

Of the four saints to whom Sussex may lay claim – St Wilfrid, St Lewinna, St Cuthman and St Richard – the second alone was Sussex-born, probably in the Cuckmere Valley. The preserved remains of the British virgin-martyr were held in honour at the Monastery of St Andrew, on whose site the present parish church of Alfriston, also dedicated to St Andrew, almost certainly now stands.

Built in its entirety in about 1360 in the form of a Greek cross, this fine church, with its graceful shingled broach spire and beautiful knapped flintwork, is rightly called 'the Cathedral of the Downs'. In this view from the east bank of the meandering River Cuckmere can be seen, at left, the Old Clergy House, which also dates from the fourteenth century.

The thatched, half-timbered, fourteenth-century Old Clergy House in Alfriston, carefully restored by the National Trust, is a fine example of Wealden domestic architecture of the period. The first property to have been purchased by the Trust, in 1896 for £10, this ancient dwelling place is still one of the smallest in its stewardship.

The signature oak leaves of the National Trust sign at the entrance to the Old Clergy House in Alfriston are neatly complemented by this display of spring colour in the front garden.

This red lion, a gaudily painted figurehead from a Dutch ship wrecked in Cuckmere Haven some three hundred years ago, stands at the corner of the Star Inn, one of two well-timbered hostelries that for centuries have faced each other across the narrow main street in Alfriston. It serves as an unofficial waymark for all those who look to take the South Downs Way out of the so-called 'capital of the Cuckmere Valley'. (*Al* as in altar and never as in Alfred.)

In season it becomes increasingly difficult to appreciate Alfriston's quiet charm, with tourists crowding into tea shoppes and weekenders occupying converted barns.

This rookery next-door to Drusillas Park ('the best small zoo in the South East') is home base to a number of the pests which have local farmers, literally, up in arms.

Embowered in the Downs above Litlington, in the Cuckmere Valley, Clapham House, a fine specimen of Sussex building in flint and brick, is long thought to have been the abode of Maria Fitzherbert, the illicit bride of George, Prince of Wales (later Prince Regent and King George IV). Indeed, in a book recently published by a person claiming to be descended from this famously childless couple, it is suggested that, posing as the 'Payne' family, they and their secret issue lived here the quiet, domestic life of the English gentry. It is in this unexpectedly romantic setting that one finds today L'École de Cuisine Française run by Sabine de Mirbeck-Brassart.

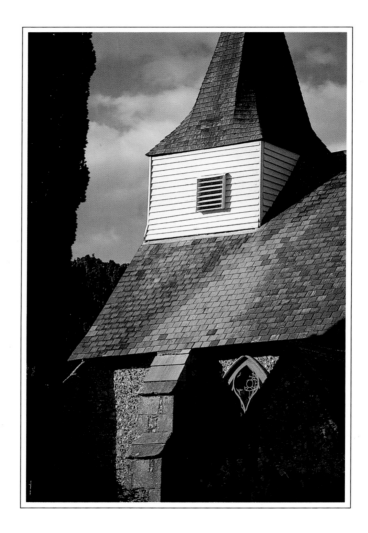

On one side bounded by the wooded Downs and on the other by wide water meadows through which the Cuckmere winds, the flint village of Litlington retains a measure of its antique integrity despite the incursion of the motor car. At the north end of this hamlet, the weatherboarded bell tower proclaims the 'little, lost Down church' of St Michael the Archangel, a building of about 1150 which was heavily restored in 1863.

The Garden House, one of the handsome dependencies of Charleston Manor, is seen to advantage in late May, framed by the laburnum flowering on a pergola recently created in the seventeen acres of gardens. Built in a fold of the Downs in about 1180 on a Saxon site, the original Norman manor house at Charleston was entered in the Domesday Book under the name of 'Cerlstone' and its owner recorded as Alured, Cup Bearer to William the Conqueror. The present dwelling, composed of Norman, Tudor and Georgian elements was characterized by Nikolaus Pevsner as 'a perfect house in a perfect setting'.

Nothing, perhaps, better captures the spirit of 'selig' Sussex – 'Holy Sussex', as the county was once known – than this grouping in the village of West Dean. While parts of the parish church of All Saints are probably Saxon, the curiously half-hipped spire that crowns the broad oblong bell tower, which John Betjeman considered unique in Sussex, is of much later date. Despite its enlargement and restoration in 1891, the Parsonage House at the south-west corner of the churchyard, built originally about 1220, is still a rare example of a small medieval dwelling, with a good claim to be the oldest inhabited rectory in England.

Much of the wildwood which originally covered Sussex has long since been destroyed by man, and before the Forestry Commission acquired over two thousand acres at West Dean, in 1926, 'no bosomed woods adorned' the surrounding Downland. Today the broad-leaved forest of Friston which has been established here increases the sense of enclosure that must have been part of the appeal of the place to King Alfred, of whose palace at the heart of the village nothing now remains.

Just about the only tangible reminder of royalty's past association with West Dean is this letter box, installed in the reign of Victoria Regina ('VR'), whose ancestor, Alfred the Great, had a palace close by.

In their march across East Sussex the South Downs are halted by two rivers: the Cuckmere and the Ouse. From the broad floor of the valley it can be seen that the River Cuckmere, once navigable up to Alfriston, where the Saxons established a sizeable settlement, was wider than it is now. The cutting of a straight channel from Exceat, in 1846, not only improved drainage but arrested the river's classic cutting of meanders, today the focal point of the Seven Sisters Country Park, an area of great scientific interest and scenic beauty, in one of the few undeveloped estuaries remaining in southern England.

The warm directional light of the sun setting behind Seaford Head throws into relief the almost ecclesiastical buttressing of Haven Brow and Short Brow, the two most westerly of the Seven Sisters. While the great landscape and wildlife importance of this coastline are recognized by its designation as Heritage Coast – it is also an Area of Outstanding Natural Beauty (AONB) and a Site of Special Scientific Importance (SSSI) – none of these protections extends below the low water mark, where a so-far voluntary scheme, the Seven Sisters Voluntary Conservation Area, exists to protect the unique marine environment.

'Snake River', the alternative name for the Cuckmere, seems particularly appropriate when the meanders are seen at sunset from the hill above Exceat. With respect to the name 'Cuckmere', a Saxon word meaning 'fast-flowing water', E.V. Lucas, the turn-of-the-century authority on Sussex folk-ways, gave it as his opinion that 'the first syllable is a severe test of knowledge of Sussex'. (Cuckmere is pronounced 'Cook-meer' and Exceat 'Ekseet'.)

Scaling the Seven Sisters is a high-risk activity for both this intrepid climber and his immediate environment, because the chalk, a pure white limestone, is a very soft and friable variety of rock. Unprotected, the cliffs erode, on average, at the rate of between two-and-a-half and three feet every year.

All that remains of the Iron Age fort 282 feet above sea level on Seaford Head is a U-shaped earth bank with its open end at the cliff edge.

Always vulnerable to attack by cross-Channel raiders, the once prosperous port of Seaford was famously defended against the French, in 1545, by Sir Nicholas Pelham.

But the turning-point in the town's fortunes was made by the great storm of 1578, which diverted the outlet of the River Ouse westward to Meeching (henceforth Newhaven).

In order to augment their meagre income, the citizens of the 'decayed haven' exercised their ancient 'rights of wreck' by luring the richly laden ships making their passage under sail round Seaford's notoriously difficult headland.

Not far from this groyne marked 'FOUL SEWER OUTFALL', at Splash Point, the River Ouse once flowed into the sea beneath Seaford Head. In 485 Seaford, identified as Mercredesburn (from Welsh *môr* meaning 'sea' and *rhyd* meaning 'ford'), was almost certainly the site of a fierce, albeit indecisive, battle marking an important stage in the progressive takeover of the region by the Saxon Ælle. In 471, according to the *Anglo-Saxon Chronicle*, an invasion force under his command captured the formerly Roman provincial capital of Regnum (Chichester), putting to flight many of the native British population who were not killed. The intruders had no hesitation in regarding the people they so ruthlessly displaced as foreigners or *wealas* (Welsh).

Just north of Seaford, between Comp Hill and Rathfinny Farm, the sweet-smelling, April-flowering hawthorn arches over the track which curves round to reach the Downland crest between Firle Beacon and Bostall Hill. From there it continues past Bo Peep – a name which recurs at smuggling sites – to Selmeston, and the Weald beyond. In the days of the 'free traders' this would have been a natural route for carrying inland contraband taken ashore at Cuckmere Haven.

There has been a dramatic revival in recent years of the ancient art of thatching. However, the demand for thatchers far exceeds the supply, in part, perhaps, because there is a five-year apprenticeship. Whereas a ridge is done every ten or fifteen years, a roof needs to be rethatched only once in every twenty to twenty-five years, if it is of combed wheat reed, a hardier type of wheat grown especially for thatching (Norfolk water reed will last between sixty and seventy years). The dense weaving and fastening of reed at the ridge of the roof is the thatcher's signature. In Winton, near Alfriston, Master Thatcher Nick Cranfield puts his imprimatur on Danny cottage owned by the National Trust.

Bo Peep Farm once occupied a strategic place below the northern escarpment, where the old turnpike road which hugs the Downs intersects with the path that climbs Bostall Hill.

Harvest time approaches below the northern escarpment of the Downs near Alciston.

Barns, 'those beached whales of English architecture', as they have been called, once a common feature of the countryside, are now an endangered species. Traditionally, farm buildings were constructed with local materials by local craftsmen and had a satisfyingly close relationship to their immediate landscape. They have suffered a sad fate since the intensification of the farming process made so many of them redundant. This solid structure in the secluded hamlet of Alciston (pronounced 'Ahl-ston') has so far avoided being turned into a bijou weekend home, the lot of several other barns in the Alfriston area, where a three-bedroom conversion with two-and-a-half acres was recently advertised at £197,000.

This stupendous 170-foot-long, fourteenth-century tithe barn is a relic of Alciston Grange, once the property of wealthy Battle Abbey. One of the greatest monastic establishments ever to have been created in this country, Battle Abbey owed its existence – and its name – to the vow made by William the Conqueror amidst the carnage on Senlac Ridge, which was subsequently fulfilled when the Abbey was consecrated in 1094.

The majestic proportions of Alciston's tithe barn are clearly revealed in this partial view of the interior.

The paintings in Berwick church are notable for their incorporation of topographical elements and people from the locality in scriptural scenes. In painting *The Supper at Emmaus* for the altar, Quentin Bell modelled his two disciples on men of the Australian Air Force who were quartered in Sussex during the war. The sumptuous altar frontal was designed by Duncan Grant and worked by his mother.

The Church of St Michael and All Angels, Berwick, one of several Downland churches dedicated to the saint, stands on high ground which was sacred in pre-Christian times. The present building, of the twelfth century, owes much of its present interest to German bombing and Bishop Bell of Chichester who, instead of replacing the leaded glass in wartime, commissioned a decorative scheme from the artist Duncan Grant. Painted on plasterboard and then fixed into position, the 'murals' – by Grant, Vanessa Bell (no relation to the Bishop) and her children, Quentin and Angelica, who all lived at nearby Charleston Farm, constitute a quirky memorial to Bloomsbury.

At Charleston, a professional and emotional partnership unique in the history of twentieth-century art and letters flourished to form an authentic masterpiece. Using this simple Sussex farmhouse as their canvas, the painters Vanessa Bell and Duncan Grant employed pictures, fabrics, pottery, doors, walls and fireplaces as elements in a composition that is, in the words of Professor Quentin Bell, who grew up there, at once 'a monument and a delight'. In his studio, depicted here, Grant is remembered in an unpublished memoir by Professor Bell as 'more serious than anywhere else in the world and capable of being very much alone in a kind of private universe where there was just him and the thing he was painting'.

Although remarkable for its interior decoration, Charleston also rejoices in having the 'apotheosis of the traditional English cottage garden', in which, if Duncan Grant's contribution was important, the presiding spirit was that of Vanessa Bell. While the great elms which marched behind the west and northern walls fell prey to the Dutch disease, and many of the sculptures which provided focal points have also gone, the garden has been lovingly restored, by Sir Peter Shepheard, with the generous assistance of the late Lila Acheson Wallace, co-founder of *Reader's Digest*, to reflect the period of intense cultivation which began with the onset of the war in 1939, when Vanessa became a full-time resident here.

The promise of renewal which, by definition, is fulfilled in every garden, can be experienced at Charleston in early May when the fruit trees blossom amidst a sea of forget-me-nots. Perhaps out of deference to Charleston's protective neighbour, the lumpy outline of the box hedge mirrors the close-cropped contours of the Downs.

It is sometimes hard to decide whether it is better to be in the Weald at some vantage point from which one can behold the long line of the South Downs swinging across the horizon from east to west, or to stand on some part of the Downs themselves and enjoy the vista from there. This view of the patchwork quilt of the Weald from Firle Beacon partly discloses Charleston, the old farmhouse on the Firle estate which, for half a century, from 1916, provided shelter and subject-matter for painters Duncan Grant and Vanessa Bell, and was the favourite resort of a number of other 'Bloomsberries'.

The primeval forest cover was originally cleared for grazing animals by Neolithic man, and for centuries the well-drained chalk grassland of the South Downs, dominated by sheep, was one of the richest habitats for plants in Europe. The sheep kept the sward in ecological balance. If an incipient hawthorn is not nipped out by a sheep's incisors at two inches, it can become a burgeoning bush within three years and part of a ground-smothering carpet scrub within five. The reduction of the chalk grassland to an estimated 5 per cent makes conservation, preferably by grazing sheep, essential. This great servant of wildlife and mother of two is quite at home on the Downs near Firle Beacon.

Round Hill Plantation below Firle Beacon. On the ridge are more than fifty early Bronze Age bowl barrows.

A Gothick eye-catcher on its lowly eminence beneath the Beacon, Firle Tower was built in 1819 by the fourth Viscount Gage to accommodate the gamekeeper on the Firle estate. Together with a companion structure at Laughton, the tower played a vital role in the local communications network: at a certain point in the train journey from London, Lord Gage's valet would lower the compartment window and wave a handkerchief to signify the approach of the master to a waiting household. A flag run up the flagpole on one or other of the two towers would then alert his lordship's coachman to proceed forthwith to Glynde railway station.

From the battlemented roof of Firle Tower one can look out over the park to the 'noble cone' of Mount Caburn. A number of fine specimen trees at Firle were damaged or destroyed in the hurricane of October 1987 and the winter storms of January 1990. Of the 15 million trees destroyed in England in 1987 about 2.8 million were in East Sussex. (The majority of this timber was in commercially managed forests and woodlands.)

Set in its own park and sheltered by the northern escarpment of the neighbouring Downs, Firle Place presides over a peaceful and still largely feudal community, as it has done since the Gage family built their first house here in about 1487. The process of classicizing the ancestral mansion was begun by Sir William Gage who, inheriting in 1713, began by pulling down and replacing the entire north-east front. Although it is not known for certain who designed the two-and-a-half storey building of Caen stone, with its hipped roof, dormers, and Venetian window surmounting the rusticated central archway in the east front, it is surmised that the mason was Arthur Morris of Lewes, who was employed by Bishop Trevor at nearby Glynde Place.

Only in the south elevation of Firle Place, viewed here from the Pleasure Grounds, can be seen what little remains of the external features of the original fifteenth-century courtyard house.

At play in the fields of the Firle estate. Only a hundred years ago between two-thirds and three-quarters of all the land in Great Britain and Ireland was owned by the aristocracy.

The weather-vane at the top of the thirteenth-century tower of St Peter in Firle was recently replaced as part of the restoration of the roof following damage done by the winter storms of January 1990. There is an unbroken record of some sixty parsons since 1325, and there was probably a place of worship here before the Norman Conquest. Throughout the Middle Ages the church was the centre for all village occasions, religious and secular, the parson teaching not only religion but such learning and culture as there was.

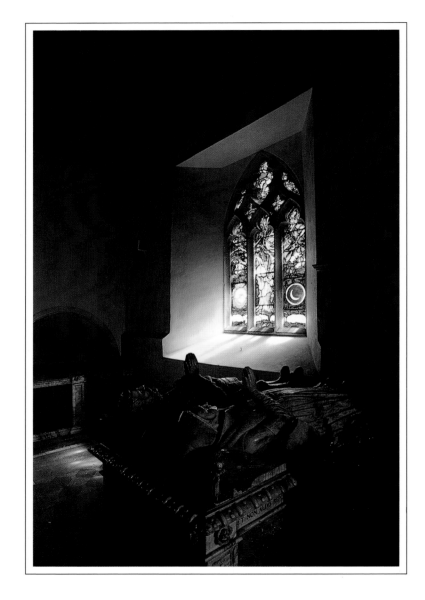

The greatest treasures of Firle church are in the sepulchral chapel of the Gage family: alabaster recumbant effigies of Sir John Gage, KC, and his wife, Philippa Guldeford, were designed and executed by Garat Johnston (or Geraert Jannsen), whose original drawings are preserved in the Firle Muniments. Sir John, a close friend of Henry VIII and Constable of the Tower, died in 1557, leaving a will, also preserved, which gives a unique picture of life at Firle in his day. The glorious window, designed by John Piper and entitled 'A Homage to William Blake's Book of Job', was installed in 1985 in memory of The Rt Hon Henry Rainald, Sixth Viscount Gage, KCVO, who succeeded to the Viscountcy in his seventeenth year, in 1912, and died in 1982.

From the top of the church tower the Revd Canon Horace James Woodward, who has since retired from his post as Vicar of Firle, was spotted taking advantage of a sunny interval between April showers to catch up on the news of the day. The dog would have preferred it if his master had played ball.

In the garden in front of his cottage, at sunset, a long-term Firle resident snatches forty winks, while his Jack Russell terrier, always on the alert, poses for the photographer.

Having cast about for a place in the country on the orders of her doctors, Virginia Woolf discovered Firle and, early in 1911, decided to rent 'a very ugly villa', which she renamed 'Little Talland House'. From there, on 8 April, she wrote to her sister, Vanessa Bell, 'The country is so amazingly beautiful, that I frequently have to stop and say "Good God!"' Until the coming of the motor car, the self-contained hamlet had a blacksmith, a miller, a tailor, a bootmaker, a butcher, a baker and a harness maker. It is not too fanciful to suppose that a connection with the neighbourhood which was to last for the rest of her life was begun by Virginia, shortly after her arrival in the village, with a visit to Firle Stores.

The Ram Inn, a seventeenth-century free house, is the only one of four public houses in Firle to have survived the closing of the old turnpike road through the village in 1812 in favour of the present highway to Eastbourne (a ram is the Gage crest). Outside, the South Downsmen, performing a Morris dance rich in symbolism, flick their handkerchiefs 'in the eye of the devil'. Most dances performed in Sussex derive from the Cotswold tradition, rooted in pagan fertility rituals, only formalized about five hundred years ago, and rescued from oblivion by Cecil Sharp at the turn of the century. The ground is struck to 'wake it up', and sticks are clashed to scare away evil spirits from the growing crops.

Marriages, christenings and funerals have been solemnized on the site of St Andrew's, Beddingham, since long before the building of the present church, whose tower, in chequered flint and sandstone, dates from about 1540. Miss Tamsin Powter, a local girl, and Senor José Luis Valero Palomares were married in the church on 4 August 1990. The young couple now live in Guadalajara.

The northern escarpment of the South Downs seen from near Trevor Gardens in late June.

Loover Shaw, a curious bump of chalk between Firle and Glynde, presents an idyllic picture; on the other, western, side of the hill, the quarrying of Balcombe Pit has removed much of this natural feature, scarring the landscape in the process.

Mill House, a private residence of dignified character, is seen from the Eastbourne-Lewes road sheltering beneath Mount Caburn.

Hung out to dry in a good southwester, a line of washing at Trevor Gardens, near Glynde, takes on the swelling form of Mount Caburn in the background.

The cricket pitch at Glynde is beautifully situated between Mount Caburn and Glynde Reach.

Navigable until quite recently, Glynde Reach today provides a quiet retreat for nesting pairs of swans.

Built on a spur of Mount Caburn, probably on the site of an earlier mansion, Glynde Place is an Elizabethan house built of Caen stone and local flint. The doorway in the quadrangle behind the gabled west front bears the date 1569 and the arms and initials of William Morley, who participated in the boom in the Wealden iron industry in the mid-sixteenth century. The fine beech trees are survivors of the hurricane of 15–16 October 1987, the greatest natural disaster to have hit East Sussex since the Great Storm of 1703.

In the archives of the East Sussex Record Office, at the Maltings in Lewes, are the original designs for the front elevation of Bishop Trevor's new stable wing, a drawing of the cupola, and day bills for work done at Glynde Place by masons, bricklayers, carpenters, plasterers, glaziers and painters. As part of the recent restoration of the clocktower, the dome was resurfaced with six tons of cast lead. Cast on a bed of sand and weighing between seven and eight pounds per square foot – twice as heavy and twice as expensive as milled lead – cast lead is made at only two places in the United Kingdom.

The cupola and clock as they appeared immediately after the restoration of the tower of the stable block at Glynde Place.

No single owner of Glynde Place did as much to change the appearance of the old Morley mansion as Bishop Trevor, the owner from 1743 to 1771 and a collateral ancestor of the present proprietor the Rt Hon Viscount Hampden. Having turned the house around to face the east, he also made a new approach through an imposing range of stables to the south, built in 1753–6, probably by John Morris of Lewes. Flanked by massive yew hedges, the drive passes under a pedimented central archway of red brick surmounted by a cupolaed clocktower of wood, through two monumental gatepiers topped with lead wyverns.

The pair of lead wyverns at Glynde Place, for which Bishop Trevor paid £48 5s. in 1759, were made by John Cheere, a popular manufacturer of garden figures, whose yard near Hyde Park Corner also turned out statuary for Stourhead. Symbolic of malice, the Trevor heraldic wyvern is a composite fictitious two-legged beast of the dragon species. A forerunner of the wyvern, the dragon of Wessex, was carried into battle on Senlac Ridge, not far from here, by Harold Godwinson, on St Calixtus's Day, 14 October 1066.

An elegant visual component of Bishop Trevor's classicizing of the landscape at Glynde is the chapel-like replacement of the existing parish church of St Mary the Virgin in 1763–5. The design by Sir Thomas Robinson Bart, who built an exactly similar church at his home at Rokeby, Yorkshire, incorporates a pedimented porch, a pediment enclosing the Bishop's mitred achievement, and a bell-cote.

Beneath a table-top tomb in the lee of this oblong Palladian edifice rest the remains of John Ellman (1753–1832), the model gentleman farmer by whom 'the breed of South Down sheep was first improved and thro his exertions spread over the whole kingdom'.

A field of rape on Home Farm, Glynde, in early April, adds its garish hue to the once quiet Downland canvas.

Red, white and blue: a patch of poppies on Mount Caburn patriotically complements the prevailing colours of a day in June.

Looking east from the shoulder of Mount Caburn, one has a view, at once majestic and simple, of Firle Beacon and, beyond it, Windover Hill, two of the highest points on the northern slope of the Downs. Also clearly visible, above Glynde, is the environmentally unfriendly working of Balcombe Pit. 'Perhaps I may be singular in my opinion,' wrote Gilbert White in a much quoted passage (*The Natural History of Selborne*, Letter 56), 'but I never contemplate these mountains without thinking I perceive somewhat analogous to growth in their gentle swellings and smooth fungus-like protuberances, their fluted sides and regular hollows and slopes, that carry at once the air of vegetative dilatation and expansion . . .'.

Many of the region's prehistoric sites are worth a visit, not only for their archaeological interest but also for their excellence as vantage-points. From the Iron Age fort on Mount Caburn there are panoramic views of the surrounding Downland. The northern escarpment of the main line of hills, from which the Caburn is curiously isolated, is strongly embayed by combs which are believed to have been produced by nivation in glacial or periglacial conditions. To the left of Ellman's Combe a bostal – an old Sussex name for a hill path – can be seen climbing to the top of Beddingham Hill.

To the north of the fortified summit of Mount Caburn lies Saxon Down, another peak in this separate block of Downland. The wide, flat-bottomed ditch was part of the new defences of the Iron Age hilltop enclosure that were added in the first half of the first century AD, possibly in response to the Roman invasion. Although their landing-place is a matter of conjecture, it is known that a force consisting of four legions plus auxiliaries – a total of perhaps 40,000 men – set sail from Boulogne in AD 43. Evidence of a fire at about that time suggests that this strongly defended site came under Roman attack and may have been compulsorily abandoned.

On the shoulder of Mount Caburn the bare chalk is exposed beneath an April sky. Gilbert White, who travelled from his home in Hampshire across the Downs to visit his aunt, Rebecca Snooke, in Ringmer, wrote that, notwithstanding an acquaintance of 'upwards of thirty years, yet still I investigate that chain of majestic mountains with fresh admiration year by year, and I think I see new beauties every time I traverse it.'

The defensive position of Lewes (from 'hlaew', Old English for 'hill') was recognized by William the Conqueror's gift of the Rape of Lewes, one of the six administrative divisions of Sussex, to William de Warenne, a specially trusted adherent, whose wife, Gundrada, was once thought, erroneously, to have been the King's daughter. Of all the land in England surveyed in the Domesday Book, about a fifth was held directly by the greater followers of the Conqueror who, at strategic points in his new kingdom, at once endowed with compact blocks of territory those members of the Norman nobility who were most deeply committed to his cause. Lewes castle was built immediately after the take-over.

A party of young visitors to
Lewes Castle take a welcome
break from the rigours of learning
about 1066 and all that.

Using large blocks of local
chalk, the Normans
constructed two mottes on the
ridge that rises steeply above the
west bank of the Ouse, where the
river penetrates the South Downs
some seven miles from the sea. On
these artificial mounds, by about
1100, they built shell keeps of flint
– also local, of course. Visible
from miles around is the only
survivor of these two defensive
strongpoints, to which flanking
polygonal towers were added in
the thirteenth century. Following
the extinction of the ruling de
Warenne family in the direct line,
in 1439, the castle, which was
their *caput*, or seat of government,
fell into decay. In the eighteenth
century, the keep, suitably
Gothicized, served as a summer
house.

While the fourteenth-century barbican of Lewes Castle is in an excellent state of preservation, subsequent changes have perhaps tended to soften the formidable nature of this structure. Before the building up of the roadway, at right, and the draining of the moat, now a lawn, the only means of access to the castle was a drawbridge. The barbican superseded the original Norman gatehouse, which can be seen at left.

The Barbican, an outer gateway protecting the bailey, was the last part of Lewes castle to be built, and is considered to be one of the finest of its kind in the country. Built of knapped flints and dressed sandstone, it incorporates all the defensive features that were state-of-the-art in the fourteenth century: drawbridge; gates; portcullis; cross-shaped arrow loops; bartizans (projecting turrets) and machicolations (projecting parapets with holes in the floor through which missiles could be dropped). Flint, 'that intractable stone' present in the upper layers of the chalk formation, was not only knapped, or split open, but squared, before being laid in fairly regular courses.

Lewes is notable for the variety and the quality of its architecture, fair testimony to the early importance and continuing prosperity of this busy port and flourishing administrative and social centre. The handsome heterogeneity of the town's building stock is evident in this view from the rounded archway of the early Norman guardhouse to the stuccoed façade of Castlegate House (c.1830), with its Doric columned porch and elegant cast-iron lampholders.

The Crown Courts building in Lewes, originally County Hall, was built between 1808 and 1812 in the neo-classical style. Inset in the Portland stone, on the second floor, are three high relief panels made of Coade stone, representing Wisdom, Justice and, seen here, Mercy. Coade stone, a kind of terracotta, was much in vogue for about fifty years following the opening, in 1769, at Pedlar's Acre, Lambeth, of a manufactory for artificial stone by Mrs Eleanor Coade. A remarkable businesswoman, Mrs Coade emphasized in her advertisements the principal selling-point of her product: 'a property peculiar to itself of resisting the frost and consequently of retaining that sharpness in which it excels every kind of stone sculpture'. Her secret formula, always closely guarded, is now lost.

Many of the old substantial residences in the High Street and adjoining thoroughfares were town houses of the local nobility and gentry, a circumstance that was noted with approval by the visiting Daniel Defoe, who rapturously described Lewes as occupying 'the most romantic situation I ever saw'. Shelleys Hotel, formerly 'The Vine', re-fronted in 1577 by Thomas Pelland, was from 1663 the residence of the Shelley family. Prominent in the political affairs of Lewes, and of Sussex, this branch of the family became extinct in the male line with the death, in 1811, of Henry Shelley, Esq.

It was first realized that giant reptiles or dinosaurs ruled the world for 140 million years in the 1820s, when Dr Gideon Mantell, a fashionable Lewes *accoucheur* and amateur paleontologist, dug Iguanadon teeth out of a Sussex quarry and published his findings in *Fossils of the South Downs*. Appropriately, it was at Castle Place, the house at 165–7 High Street with the punning ammonite capitals added by Amon Wilds, purchased by Mantell, that the famous geological collections later acquired by the British Museum were displayed. Wilds was the architect most responsible for Regency Brighton, a watering place made fashionable by Dr Richard Russell, another famous Lewes physician.

The London train brings summer visitors to Lewes station (1885).

The national festival commemorating the defeat of a Popish plot in 1605 has traditionally been celebrated with extra fervour in Lewes, whose famous Bonfire Societies annually process the length of the High Street on Guy Fawkes night. Between 1555 and 1557, seventeen men and women were burned at the stake here as part of Queen Mary's fanatical campaign to re-establish the authority of the Pope. One of the greatest figures in the history of popular struggle, Tom Paine, who lived in a house just off the High Street, said, 'I believe religious duties consist in doing justice, loving mercy and endeavouring to make our fellow citizens happy. My own mind is my church, and to do good is my religion.'

This richly carved keystone, representing Dionysus or a follower of the god of wine, is part of the superabundant detail of the Town Hall in Lewes, a red brick structure of Victorian vintage, which stands near the site of the infamous sixteenth-century autos-da-fé. It is said that the medieval cellars of the building were used to confine the martyrs prior to their public execution.

Ironically, it was the cutting of the Brighton and Hastings Railway right across the church and cloister of the long neglected ruins of the Cluniac Priory of St Pancras in Southover that helped give people a new awareness of their ancient heritage. There was great excitement during the excavations when, on 28 October 1845, the discovery was made of leaden cists containing the bones of William de Warenne and his wife, Gundrada, joint founders, in 1077, of one of the most magnificent monasteries England ever possessed. The formation, in 1845, of the Sussex Archaeological Society may be credited to Gundrada, of whom it is said on her exquisitely carved black Tournai marble tombstone that 'She introduced the balm of good manners into the English churches'.

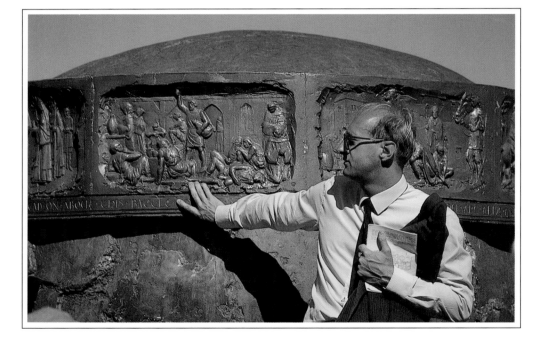

Doubling in the most delightfully unexpected fashion as the town's unofficial historiographer, Dr Graham Mayhew, the Mayor of Lewes, goes walk-about to interpret its rich heritage for the benefit of visitors. The Battle of Lewes Memorial, a gift to the people of Lewes in 1964, stands in the grounds of the priory in Southover. It was here, in 1364, at Henry III's headquarters, following the king's defeat by Simon de Montfort, that the signing of the Mise of Lewes took place. This event, as Dr Mayhew explains, is often cited as the beginning of parliamentary government in this country.

On a hot summer's day in Lewes, the bright paintwork of these house-fronts on Priory Street, Southover, has the refreshing appeal of Neapolitan ices.

Southover, the gracious old suburb of the county town of Lewes, is distinguished by a quantity of superior architecture, and is at its grandest in Priory Crescent, a Regency survival. Employing to good effect both stucco and so-called white brick (not common in Lewes but popular elsewhere in the first half of the nineteenth century), John Blaker, the developer, and George Harman, a local mason, made an imposing addition to the townscape, all of twenty bays long.

From 1630 to 1637 John Evelyn, the future diarist and horticulturist attended the priory school, founded in Southover in 1512 (moved in 1714; now the grammar school), and made his home at Southover Grange, which was built in 1572 with Caen stone taken from the ruins of the demolished St Pancras's Priory nearby. The gardens that surround the much altered Elizabethan house, with their colourful bedding displays and magnificent old trees, are one of the great amenities of Lewes today.

Noted for its double herbaceous border, the garden of Offham House, one of several beautiful and historic gardens in East Sussex, is among the approximately 2,500 private gardens which are open to the public on a limited basis under the National Gardens Scheme Charitable Trust. Offham House, the property of Anne and Sandy Goodman, is a Queen Anne residence of 1676, situated under the Downs some two miles north of Lewes.

The Ouse Valley rejoices in a number of churches of great antiquity, among them the sturdy survivor of an age of faith which shelters beneath the Downs at Kingston. This house of worship is somewhat unusual in that it was dedicated to St Pancras, a distinction that at one time was shared with a church in nearby Southover. Under the patronage of the de Warrenes, the church in Southover was the nucleus of the Priory of St Pancras, one of the greatest monastic establishments in the country.

'It's wonderful how large these low hills seem when you're on them', wrote G.K. Chesterton (*Father Brown Stories*), who might have been standing beneath this billowing cloud on Iford Hill when he was moved to describe the South Downs in this fashion. In his classic study, *Nature in Downland*, W.H. Hudson developed the theme: 'Once we have got above the world, and have an unobstructed view all round, whether the height above the surrounding country be 500 or 5,000 feet, then we at once experience all that sense of freedom, triumph and elation which the mind is capable of.'

The parish church of St John, Piddinghoe (pronounced 'Pidd'n'oo' locally), with its Sussex 'fool's cap' spire, is one of only three churches, all in the Ouse valley, with circular flint towers of late twelfth- or early thirteenth-century date (the other two are at Lewes and Southease). The church's enchanting setting on a little hill on a bend in the river has been compromised in recent years by the unconscionable building, in unsympathetic materials, of a house on the bank below. The salmon-trout weather-vane, which Kipling transmuted into a 'begilded dolphin', still surmounts the shingled octagonal spire.

C lose to one million passengers a year use the cross-Channel ferry to Dieppe from Newhaven, the only port in Sussex which has such a service. 'Of Newhaven,' it has been well said, by E.V. Lucas, 'there is little to say, except that in rough weather the traveller from France is very glad to reach it, and on a fine day the traveller from England is happy to leave it behind'. Two travellers from France who must have been very glad to reach Newhaven, on 3 March 1848, were King Louis-Philippe and his Queen, who checked into the Bridge Hotel as 'Mr and Mrs William Smith', following their escape from terminally rough weather in Paris.

T he unfrequented road from Southease to Telscombe winds its way over the Downs past Fore Hill.

This subtopian sprawl, on the other side of Telscombe Cliffs from Peacehaven, is typical of the development which has been permitted on the once open Downland between Rottingdean and Newhaven since Charles Neville bought a tract of land and, in 1919, started to build what he promised would be an attractive seaside garden city. Now the whole coastline has been made into a kind of seaside slum, a hopelessly ugly agglomeration of mean, squat bungalows. It was to oppose all such invasions of our natural heritage and to conserve the little of it that remains unspoilt that the Society of Sussex Downsmen was formed in 1923.

Not far from the madding crowd, unspoilt Telscombe Tye reaches back from the cliffs near Rottingdean to embrace the village of Telscombe, hidden in a secluded hollow high on the Downs. There, for over eight hundred years, on an earlier Saxon site, has stood the church of St Laurence, its Norman nave and chancel anchoring the stone-cornered flint tower surmounted by a 'Sussex cap'. Both the village and the surrounding land owe their preservation to Ambrose Goreham, a wealthy, retired bookmaker, who bequeathed his considerable holdings in Telscombe to Brighton Council, so that it might be protected from development. Goreham also restored the church, to celebrate the success of his horse, Shannon Lass, in the Grand National of 1902.

Made by William Morris from the designs of Sir Edward Burne-Jones, the seven stained-glass windows in the parish church of St Margaret, Rottingdean are acknowledged to be some of their finest work. The three-light east window, representing the three archangels, Gabriel, Michael and Raphael, of which this panel depicting Michael slaying the dragon forms part, was given by the great pre-Raphaelite painter to commemorate the marriage of his daughter Margaret in the church, and was installed in 1893. Among the family members who kept vigil in the church when Burne-Jones died five years later was his nephew, Rudyard Kipling. From 1897 to 1902 the arch-celebrant of the South Downs made his own home in Rottingdean, writing some of his most enduring work here.

One of the principal figures, the Archangel Gabriel, represented in the sublime three-light east window by Burne-Jones and Morris that is Rottingdean's greatest treasure.

Isolated on its hill overlooking the village of Brighthelmstone, the church of St Nicolas of Myra, patron saint of seafarers, was a landmark for local fishermen and the French raiders who so frequently crossed the English Channel. Unlike the church in Rottingdean which, in 1377, was burned with the people in it, St Nicolas emerged unscathed when the village was sacked by the French in 1514 and 1545. Having survived severe storms in the early eighteenth century, the church was remorselessly restored in the 1850s, only to lose its status as parish church in 1873. In the early days of Brighton's emergence as a seaside resort the fourteenth-century tower was topped by a weather-vane in the form of a fish.

Among the extraordinary number of fine churches to be found in Brighton, is the church of St Peter, which succeeded St Nicolas's as parish church. Built between 1824 and 1828 to the design of Sir Charles Barry, St Peter's represents not only one of the earliest but also one of the finest examples of the Gothic Revival.

Trailing debts of half a million, and accompanied by his secret and illegal morganatic bride, the twice-widowed, comely, Catholic Maria Fitzherbert, who was five years his senior, the 23-year-old George, Prince of Wales (the future Prince Regent and King George IV) came to Brighton, for his third season, in 1785. 'Prinny's' passion for 'Mrs Fitz' was matched in intensity only by his 35-year-long obsession with building, in progressively more exotic fashion, his 'Marine Pavilion'. In all, during his lifetime, George spent a grand total of £502,797 6s 10d on the estate, buildings and furnishings of the celebrated seaside palace which, in its final form, dating from 1815–22, is a curiously beautiful confection, by John Nash, of Indian, Chinese and Persian styles.

While the Prince of Wales may have been drawn to Brighton for a second season in 1784 by the angelic figure of a sea-nymph whom he one day encountered reclining on one of the groynes of the beach, when he began to build his 'Marine Pavilion', in 1786, he oriented it to overlook the Steine, even arranging to view the fashionable throng in a mirror placed over his bed. Royal Crescent, built between 1798 and 1810, on the cliff east of the Pavilion, was, according to Pevsner, 'the earliest demonstration of a sympathy with sea and beach'. Thereafter, 'Regency' terraces and squares sprang up along the front, giving Brighton that aristocratic *cachet* which it has not quite succeeded in losing.

First allowed to decay, then made the victim of a protracted, unseemly and, so far, inconclusive squabble over funding for its restoration, the 1,115-foot Great West Pier, constructed of harmoniously wrought and cast iron between 1863 and 1866 by the Victorian visionary Eugenius Birch, is today a crumbling monument to the shortsighted management of our collective past. In its heyday, this outstanding example of marine architecture (one of two such structures in Brighton) was the expression of the English ruling passion for the seaside, something that may be said to have started, c.1754, with the opening on the front, by Dr Richard Russell, a Lewes physician, of an establishment for seawater bathing.

Intrepid windsurfers today show off their prowess where a couple of hundred years ago phlegmatic Brits had to be persuaded of the therapeutic value of exposure to sea water by means of bathing machines operated by local fisherfolk-turned-'dippers'. Brighton's great concentration of elegant housing, which dates from this happy discovery in the late eighteenth century has been all but crowded out in recent years by such behemoths as can be seen here dominating the waterfront.

The manor of Brighthelmstone-Atlingworth was mentioned in the Domesday Book (1086), its population given as 90, and the annual rent paid as 4,000 herrings. Subsequent acts of God and the French between them succeeded in laying waste the medieval fishing village, and all that remains to suggest its original layout are the snaking streets and narrow alleyways that honeycomb the area between North Street and the sea known as 'the Lanes'. Here, high fashion flowers alongside second-hand rose.

Finding no beauty in the bare outlines of the Downs which, in the 1770s, were much more visible behind Brighton, Dr Johnson complained to his friends the Thrales, with whom he stayed on West Street, that the place was 'so truly desolate that if one had a mind to hang oneself for desperation at being obliged to live there, it would be difficult to find a tree on which to fasten the rope'. One wonders to what lengths the author of the remark that 'the man who is tired of London is tired of life' would be driven by this prospect of 'London-on-Sea', as Brighton has come to be known.

East Sussex was an isolated area until the great era of road building from the 1790s and the coming of the railways in the 1840s. Around 1820 about fifty coaches ran daily between London and Brighton, and more than a dozen 'packets' operated services to France. The opening of the railway line from the capital to the resort, marked by the arrival of the first train from London, on 21 September 1841, accelerated the pace of local development. In 1821 Brighton had a population of 24,429; by 1851 the number had grown to 65,569.

Always vulnerable to attack from the Continent, Brighton is heavily invaded each summer by battalions of English-language students.

This October sowing of seed on the Downland in back of Brighton, near Falmer, sets off a feeding frenzy among the local population of sea gulls.

If it is true, as it is often asserted, that a picture is worth a thousand words, it should be pointed out that in the case of this image only half the story is therein told. This idyllic scene of the village pond at Falmer in the spring contains no hint of the fact that in the sixties the village was partitioned – and the life of the centuries-old community cut short – when a major road was driven right through its heart.

To get to Stanmer village, where this flint and brick cottage is located, one has to drive through the 200-acre wooded park that was laid out by the Pelham family around the Palladian mansion that they built for themselves in the 1720s. Stanmer Park was acquired by Brighton Corporation in 1947, and the village is now a rural museum.

At the outdoor café in the village of Stanmer, this equine customer appears to be uncertain whether to phone in his order or rely on the hospitality of strangers.

A dairy herd forms a major part of the model farm at Stanmer.

Under the supervision of Mark Hayward, the ranger for the eight square miles of Brighton-Hove Downland behind Hangleton, a new stile is built on Benfield Hill.

It is distressing to observe the disfiguring of the Downland by 'mad car disease'. The controversial Brighton/Hove Bypass, viewed here in the Hangleton to Dyke Road stretch from the top of Red Hill, carves eight-and-a-half miles of dual carriageway mainly out of the South Downs, forever impairing our precious visual heritage and reducing the already finite number of wildlife habitats. Despite the fact that motor vehicles are responsible for more air pollution than any other source, one million more cars are added each year to the 19 million now on the roads, to make way for which, up to 4,000 acres of rural land annually are being destroyed.

INDEX